Art in the Woods

Written by Elizabeth Galloway
Photographed by Tim Platt

Collins

You can find lots of things in a wood.

3

Collect things to make your own wood.

4

Take your things home.

Get ready.

Cut out the side and back of a box.

Stick the twigs and leaves on.

8

Make leaf rubbings.

Stick the paper on.

Paint the pine cones.

Stick the pine cones on.

Now you've made a wood.

Making a wood

🐾 Ideas for reading 🐾

Written by Clare Dowdall, PhD
Lecturer and Primary Literacy Consultant

Learning objectives: children read and understand simple sentences; children follow instructions involving several ideas or actions; children are confident to try new activities; they talk about the features of their own immediate environment

Curriculum links: Expressive arts and design: Exploring and using media and materials

High frequency words: in, the, to, make, you, can, of, a, get, and, your, on, now, made

Interest words: wood, collect, take, cut, side, back, box, stick, twigs, leaves, make, leaf, rubbings, paper, paint, pine cones

Resources: a collection of leaves for rubbing and sticking, sticks, pine cones, thick wax crayons, poster paints, paintbrushes, scissors, PVA glue, white tack, a large cereal box, books about trees

Word count: 58

Getting started

- Ask children, *who has been to the woods?* Hand out the books and look at the photograph on the front cover. Help children to describe what it is like in the woods, using their senses, e.g. what they can see, hear, smell and feel.

- Ask children to read the title aloud. Look at the word *art* and practise reading it.

- Turn to the blurb. Ask children to read the blurb aloud. Discuss what this instruction book will describe, e.g. how to make art from things that are found in the woods.

Reading and responding

- Turn to pp2–3. Read the text and ask what the children might find in the woods.

- Turn to pp4–5. Look at the pictures and read the text together. Check that children understand what the girl and boy in the book are doing.